A Home for
Lonely Souls

D1717911

Amazon Self-Publishing
Kindle Direct Publishing

Fiction

God is a Woman
Far From Heaven

Poetry

Don't Wait til I Die to Love Me vol. I, II, & III
The Pisces
Songs for Each Mood II
Don't Wait Til I Die to Love Me
Nirvana: Pieces of Self-Healing vol. 1 & 2
Young Heart, Old Soul
Songs for Each Mood
A Day Without Sun
To Build a Home
Before I Die, I Must Say This

Collabs w/ Moonsoulchild

Self-Talks
Heal, Inspire, Love

Follow the Author

Tiktok: MichaelTavon

Instagram: ByMichaelTavon

Twitter: MichaelTavon

Apple Music & Spotify: Michael Tavon

A Home for Lonely Souls

Michael Tavon

Cheers to You

Your whole world seems
To be falling apart
But after the smoke clears
You'll realize that
Everything must go
For your new life
To fall in place

The angst you feel
Aches so deeply
But you have the strength
To smile again
And the pain will fade

The universe has been testing
Your faith,
And you still haven't given up.
So, cheers to you
For surviving another day

<u>In The End (Remix)</u>

One day, I will leave my fears
One day, I will swallow my pride
One day, I will study my tears
To learn why I hide from my
Inner child

Someday, I will let go of the past
Someday, I will find my true bliss

'Cause my heart's been heavy
For too long
There must be a place better
than this

I'm gonna find home
   I'm gonna find home
      my little heaven on earth

I'm gonna find home
   I'm gonna find home
     It's not who I used to be
     It's about who I'll become,
        In the end

A Home for Lonely Souls

A new place to call home
A new place to be free
A new place to feel warm
A new place to sleep at ease

One day, this work will bloom
Into something fruitful
One day this life will be beautiful

A harmonious life like music
Because for so long,
My days have been dull
I'm so eager to meet my new home

I'm gonna find home
  I'm gonna find home
    my little heaven on earth

I'm gonna find home
  I'm gonna find home
    It's not who I used to be
    It's about who I'll become,
      In the end

Prayer I

Dearly heavenly,

As I lay to rest, I pray my spirit gets replenished with patience. I carry so much worry when daylight arrives; my body is empty by night. Time is my worst enemy; I'm too young to be this incredibly tired. Constantly remind me to be gentle with myself when it slips my mind. When I feel lost, redirect me to my purpose, so I can feel at ease when the stars align. When this journey gets dark, allow the streetlights to shine so they can keep me from feeling like I'm not too far from where I belong. Provide the security I need to feel safe on this journey.

Amen.

Sunken Place

When I was clawing from a sunken hole
Of sorrow and confusion,
Slowly losing sight of the future,
I needed you to pull me up,
Instead, you threw dirt in my plot
To stop me from reaching the top,

My heart pumped bitter blood
Whenever I heard your name
When I saw you
I turned the other way

Was my love just a pastime?
Is this why turning cold
Came easier than winter
To you?

But over time,
The heartache waned
Clarity arose after the fog cleared

I could no longer despise
You for choosing yourself
It wasn't your responsibility
To carry my burdens

At the time
I wish you
Didn't give up on me
I wish you had hurt me
A little bit softer

I try my best
To treat my heart with mercy
I am worthy of grace

The Problem Is

You allow them to
Step over your boundaries
Because you fear
They'll treat your
Heart like a highway
And exit
When their access to you
Gets denied

Is keeping them around
Worth losing your peace?

If standing up for yourself
Creates distance between you and them
Make sure those roads
Are closed when they decide
To drive back into your life

Love Lost

Lost love
Turned you into
a helpless romantic
Empty-hearted
and crestfallen

They broke your trust
Like a fallen vase
Because they didn't
Handle you with care,
Leaving you
With their mess
to repair

With a tear-soaked pillow
And a playlist of sad songs
You question what
you did wrong,
Somehow, it's your fault?

Their mistakes
Shouldn't be your
Burdens to bear,
If they cared,
They'd still be there

Once you realize
losing them was a blessing
In disguise
You'll lose the desire
To want them in your life

Elon

If I had a dime
For every time I doubted myself,
I'd be wealthier than Elon musk

Dial 9-8-8
(Suicide Prevention Hotline)

You've been fighting for peace
for so long
Your heart is war-torn

Happiness feels like a myth
And trying no longer makes sense

You've been playing hide n seek
With your inner child for so long,
You don't even try to find them anymore

Lost in grief,
There's no map
To guide you,
When met with a dead-end

When you convince yourself
You're unworthy of fresh air
Dial three numbers
that will save your life
 (9-8-8)

Loneliness is a feeling so fleeting.
I promise you no longer
Have to fight your internal war alone

Happy: Affirmation

My happiness is ready
To be discovered
My happiness is ready
To be claimed
When I find my bliss
I will not doubt or turn it away
Because I deserve to be happy

I need you to understand,
If you don't align
With my growth
I must let you go

Free: Affirmation

I am growing; I am healing.
I am unlearning everything
That kept me mentally enslaved
I am well on my way to
Becoming the most liberated
Version of myself

Reconnect

I'd rather grow with you

Than grow apart,

But if the universe

Doesn't align with our stars

Let's not cause emotional strain

By going against the grain

Some connections are meant to fade

But hopefully—one day

We will reconnect again

Check up on Your Friends

Sometimes the person you love is struggling before your
eyes, but you're so wrapped up in your life that you don't
see the signs. You don't hear their cries for help because
you're tone-deaf to the situation. You think they're fine,
but their smile is a disguise. Without realizing you've made
them feel more alone by not listening when their heart
speaks. There's a reason why family and friends are usually
shocked when they lose a loved one by suicide. This is not
an attempt to guilt trip you; I just want you to be more
aware, be there for them, don't wait til it's too late to care.

Talk it Out IV

My heart is a safe space,
Make it your new home
I promise you no longer have
to struggle alone

When the voices in your mind
Intensify like a stadium crowd,
Don't be afraid to talk it out
I will be there to silence the doubt

When depression gets violent
Please don't suffer in silence,
I'm here to help you fight

Never be afraid to speak
When the feeling of emptiness
Leaves you weak,
As someone who loves you
I will always help you reach
The peak

Whenever the thought
Of dying crosses your mind
Hit my line, so I can remind you
Why you deserve to be alive

<u>Safeness</u>

I want you to feel safe enough
To be real with me

Your voice is a melody,
Sing your song
So I can provide the love
You need to see

Lessen the worry
Of wasting your energy
Old pain won't turn me
into a future enemy

I would never throw cold stones
To your warm heart of glass
I understand the past
Is why you feel so safe
Behind a mask

Expose the windows
To your soul
Honesty is key
To becoming whole
My intentions are pure
My heart is gold

My depression was
a weed-smoking fiend.
A party-animal.
A sex-machine.
Third shift Netflix binger.
Sleep avoidant.
A rebel to responsibilities.
A habitual job quitter.

My depression was fun,
Under the influence
Of my own delusion
Living a reality
Diluted by lies
I didn't realize
My joy was a façade

Depression isn't always
Deep sleep, unkempt rooms,
And grief eating

Depression loves to party too

<u>To The Friend Who is Suffering</u>

Take my hand, my friend
I'll guide you to
Where you need to go
You don't have
to travel this journey alone

Your silent suffering ends today
Speak your truth to me,
And I will walk with you

Allow my love
to be the bright hues
You need
When your mood is blue

<u>Home</u>

It's not where you've been
It's where you land
When the journey ends,
So don't cut your travels short
My friend, this is where
your bliss will begin

Scene I

(The One who Fucked up)

You fucked up the greatest love to ever happened to you, and now you're stuck in regret, wishing for a mulligan, but father time offers no do-overs. Your eyes can't stand to see how much better off they are without you. It's driving you mad; no number of apologies will patch the wound you gashed through their heart with betrayal as your weapon. The truth cuts deep, now bleed. All you can do is let them go---set them free; you've done enough damage already.

<u>Haunting</u>

Your silence is the only language
gaslighters take heed to
when the guilt of mistreating you
finally haunts them.

Scene 2:

(The one who's recovering)

You miss them like hell
You're an emotional wreck now

You get an upset stomach
whenever you taste their favorite dish

You cry when their favorite songs
Play in your ear

And sleep no longer comes easy
Because resting in a half-empty bed
Doesn't feel right.

Every time you stare at the tee shirt
They left behind, you resist the urge
To return it, so you can see them
One last time.

You think closure will be the remedy
To your broken heart

Just remember the many times
they mistreated you
With no remorse,

Choosing yourself was the best decision.

Differences

You feel lonely now,

But don't sulk for too long

See this as an opportunity

To spot the difference between

The people who hold you down

And the people who hold you back

A Home for Lonely Souls

Once I grow tired of explaining myself,
silence becomes the only language
I'll speak to those
who refuse to understand me.

Hey Lonely Soul

You watch fireflies
Illuminate the night
Like constellations in the sky
And marvel at the sight of moonlight
You find solace in the simple life,

In a world where everyone goes
A thousand miles per hour
You prefer to go slow
Is this why you feel so alone?

You're a metaphor
Too complex for ordinary minds,
Impossible to replace,
You're one of a kind

You feel like an outcast
around peers
'cause your soul
Is way beyond your years

As much as you crave
to be understood
The lack thereof
Doesn't damage
Your mental health.

_**You found bliss in loneliness
The moment you
Fell in love with yourself**_

Land: Time

You're the architect
of your reality
Where time is your land;
The power to build
something special
Is in your hands

7 Signs of Depression

You loathe the idea of being alone
But push people away
when they get too close

You give in to those impulses
Created by that dark inner voice
That urges you to indulge
You give in, then suffer in utter
Remorse when it's done

You feel lost in your own home
Cramped in your room,
You have space
With nowhere to go

Your bed is a comfort zone
And you've grown content
With never leaving alone

You become hyper-defensive
And always feel personally attacked
When people offer help
You push back

Tears pour down
Your face without reason
Summer rain, winter pain
All year is crying season

Nothing seems to matter
But the vices that make you high
To mask the pain inside
Numb to reality,
Waiting to die

Prayer II

Dear Heavenly,

Please realign me with everything that feeds my soul purpose and fills my heart with peace. As of late, I've been emotionally imbalanced, and I need to reconnect with myself. Provide the mirror to my soul so I can look inward and see a reflection I'm proud of. I'm ready to be open. I'm ready to feel like myself again.

Dead Roaches

Scattered all over
The bathroom floor
I rushed to the kitchen
and saw more,

Dead roaches
rolled on their shells
I think, "This must be hell."

I asked my fiancé
To help me clean this mess
I asked God
"Why do I deserve this stress."

Anxious with a gut
Knotted with fear
The more we cleaned
The more dead roaches appeared

Saved by the alarm clock
My body rose in a shock

I googled the meaning behind
Dreams about dead roaches,

This is what I discovered

"Roaches can symbolize an evil spirit
 that intends to rob you of your peace
and well-being.
Seeing the roach as dead means
that **God has conquered
this threat and protected
you from harm**."

If that stands to be true,
Thank you, Jesus, for a job well done
For your birthday, I'll send a hallmark card

The Apology You Deserved
from the Parent Who Abused You

There's no excuse
for the damage I did,
As regret cuts through
My conscious like a knife
I need to make amends

It was never your fault
I caused all those wounds
And only poured salt,
When I was too weak to admit
I was wrong

I formed my hands
As weapons to hurt
My own flesh and blood
When you deserved to be
held and loved

I was supposed to protect you
From feeling hopeless
Instead, I became the reason
Why you're broken

I failed you a thousand times
There's no way I can repair
If you choose to not forgive me,
It's fair

It's been a while since I said this
I love you kid
I promise to God
To never hurt you again

(After 2pac's Letter To My Unborn)

Your first cries
Will be in my arms
To let you know
I'll always protect you from harm

My chest will always
Be a resting nest
When your heart feels stressed
Never suppress yo' emotions
My ears are an ocean
For you to express
The worries you soak in

This world is such a storm,
And daddy will be your shelter
To make the weather better
So never run from me

My precious seed
I'll feed you everything
You'll need to
bloom into your destiny

This letter is a prophecy
To my unborn,
You'll be the manifestation
Of all the curses I had to unlearn
You'll never burn with the concern
Of me hurting your soul

I'm working on myself
So you can get the best version
Of this person
When you set foot on earth's surface
Loving you is my purpose
And I promise
To never make you feel worthless

I know life has been rough, to say the least, but please understand this, I got you; I'll provide a shoulder to lean on when you feel you lack the strength to carry on. I promise you don't have to move mountains alone.

How people treat you is a reflection
Of the energy you project, granted there are exceptions to
the rule, but if people treat you like a footstool, maybe it's
because you allow them to walk all over you.

That Love

Find the type of love
that makes heartache irrelevant.
The type of love
that never reminds you of pain.
The kind of love
that inspires you to overcome your fears.
The kind of love
That brings your heart comfort.

Iron heart

Even when I'm morose and aloof
 I am aware that sadness
  is better than feeling numb

 This heart I possess
    Is steadfast,
Despite being worn down
From stress
It refuses to give in
To this terrible feeling

Feel Again

You can pretend
Sadness doesn't exist within you
And wear a smile to hide
The grief behind those eyes

But at what cost?
Are you willing to lose
What's left of you
To gain a false sense
Of peace?

Forcing your heart to be numb
Because you're afraid to get hurt
is an unproductive way to move on

Healing begins with diving
Into the oceans of your emotions,
With the belief of not drowning

 Open your heart
You deserve to feel again

"I'm proud of myself for getting out of bed today
and that's more than enough."

A Home for Lonely Souls

Now listening to Good Days by SZA

Getting out of bed,
a daunting chore
this mournful morning,
but I summon the strength
to set my soles to the floor.

A deep yawn bellow from
The depths of my belly
My face cringes.
breath smelly
Body's weak, knees heavy

My cloudy eyes,
on the brink of rain
A deep stretch
like I was detained
In a coffin for seventeen days

I refuse to let
the blue devil win
I'm proud of me
For getting out of bed again

Affirmation

I will begin to heal
The wounds from childhood traumas
So I can attract the life I deserve.

A Home for Lonely Souls

(One thing I've learned)

When you try to love from
The broken places in your heart
You will have a hard time
 Functioning alone,

You allow others
To treat your boundaries
Like a welcome mat
You turn a blind eye
To bright red flags
And do everything
To make them stay

You treat your heart
like poker chips
When the odds
Are stacked against you
And go all in,
Even if the risk
Isn't worth the reward

Stop trying to
Love from a broken place
Gambling with your heart
Will break you every time

The Bodyguard

When those gorgeous eyes
Seek some well-deserved rest,
My warm embrace
Will make you feel safe
Like the spirits you pray to

When I place you in my arms
You'll be protected from
Nightmares and harm

<u>For Quite Sanity</u>

Don't sing your concerns
Until your voice becomes
A broken record
When they continue
To ignore the hurt
You pour from the heart --
(You deserve to be heard)

Your boundaries
Aren't a negotiation
Cut them off if they refuse
To respect it

When tensions intensify
Like moss on trees
Never fight, yell, or cry
To get your point across, please

Silence has a falsetto
With the most soulful song
Leave softly; they'll miss you
When you're gone

One of Them Days

Every step I plant on the pavement
Is heavy labor on the knees

I feel sluggish and weak
The sunbeams
As my body begs for more sleep

A piece of me leaves
Along with every breath
I exhale

I try to inhale peace
But sadness prevails

Just one of them days,
I don't want to feel this way
But I gotta maintain

I roll with the punches,
Til the jabs bruise my ribs

Life is a film with no script
And I'm forced to Adlib

Today, I just want to stay in bed
But I gotta tread to meet
My brighter days ahead

My hugs are so tight and warm
you will feel the lilt of my heart
when I embrace you

Juxtapose

There's no place for revenge in healing. Revenge comes from a place of hurt and spite. It's a temporary fix to make you feel good in short sight, but once the feeling fades the issue still resides in your mind. Revenge is a dish best not served at all. Starve them of the idea that you're holding onto feelings long gone.

The opposite of revenge is forgiveness. Don't let them
believe they still have control over your emotions by
sending constant reminders of their poor choices.
Forgiveness is a gift --- a gesture of grace. When you
finally let go-- revenge will no longer be a mission to
chase. You'll find peace in their absence. Forgiveness is the
key to freedom.

Meet me at the Bar at 9

Loneliness is a place
Where silence and gloom meet
For cheap thrills and highs
'Til the rooster crows

In this hopeless space
the tea ain't sweet
Sober truths behind drunken cries
Melancholy blues on the dance floor

They all remember my face
We jig to the same beat,
It's so hard to say goodbye,
When dancing with my woes

Silence and gloom: we're tight like lace
They won't let me leave
Believe me, I always try
But still have a long way to go

Erasure

What happened is,
Time slowly erased
The essence of childhood,
Our temples became
a host of memories
We fear to forget

Each breath we exhale
A blessing and a curse,
A reminder of fresh life
A reminder of our mortality
Youth keeps slipping away
We should be happy
To be alive anyway

We yearn for simplicity
We crave for
A slice of blissful ignorance

Within a blink of an eye
We've grown too old for
Water balloon fights
And mud pies

Time forces us to grow up
Without our consent

The Good, The Bad, The Ugly

Keep runnin'
and those demons
will keep chasin'

A long race to nowhere
when shame & regret
joins the relay

Sit with the bad,
give those brash demons
a warm hug
the ugly needs love too

To feel good, again
Stop runnin' from the bad
When it calls

Stillness is essential to healing

When

When you reach a certain age

People begin to
Ask *when* until you lose
All sense of self-worth,
Because your answers are
Uncertain and indirect

When are you having children?
 When are you getting married?
When are you going to buy a home?
When
   when
       When are you going to find a new car
— a better paying job?
When are you going to finish school
  When
     When
       When

They anticipate your every move
The way they did
When you were a toddler
Learning how to conquer
The ground beneath you

  The only difference is,
This walk isn't the distance
of a living room
  And none is cheering
No hugs wait for you
at the finish line…

Instead, there's the pressure
Of expectations

And there's no one to help you up
When you fall

When you answer
I'm not ready; I don't know
Or I'm working on it

The silence becomes so sharp
You can feel the disappointment
Cutting the air

They ask *when*,
But never have anything to say
When you ask *How*

After a certain age, there's little guidance
You just gotta know how to do this walk alone

7 Signs that You're Falling in Love

A smile rises under your sunlit eyes like ocean tides
when their name blows like the wind.

You send good morning texts when the sunrises
to let them know they're the first thing on your mind

Your heart flutters like butterfly wings
When your phone rings,
And it's their name on the screen

You feel like the richest person in the world
When you spend time with them,
Days feel so much better
You pray you can afford to stay
In their life forever

When the sky closes, they lie next to you.
Nighttime no longer feels lonely.
A Tranquil slumber awaits,
You feel safe when those eyes shut tight.

Those around you notice a new glow in your aura,
Sorrow no longer follows when you step outside

Lastly, when they speak, your ears catch every word,
Eager to learn who they are and who they were
So you can provide the love they deserve too.

Sonder Heart

Life will go on without you
The harshest truth
Once sonder hits

Oceans will not dry
Clouds will not mourn your demise

Generations will forget about you
Over time

This realization isn't as depressing
as it seems,

Once you leave your mark,
And all else fades
You'll be set free

Today is a burden
You shouldn't carry
For too long,
Because it doesn't matter at all

Life goes on without you
And you should move on
Before you lose too much time
Sulking over the people you've lost

Hidden Gems

Good love will unearth
   The many gems hidden in your heart,
   Not bury you alive

Good love never hurts
   It's salvation, a fresh start
   To build a home and thrive

If people step on you like a staircase,
it's because you allow them to walk all over you.
Have the backbone to stand up for yourself

Faith

We're strong together
Like two palms in prayer
Such a blessing to find
Someone to trust in this
Faithless world

Ugly Shades

After living in denial
I finally opened my eyes

Those baby blue apologies
Faded into white lies

Once I saw the true colors
Behind your disguise
It was time to cut ties

I was a fool for your hues
Until those ugly shades
Came to light

My aura is too bright
to share my life
with someone who
lives in black and white

Blood Bath

Tempers flare like Florida air
No one is going without a fight
  Neither of you --- listening
   Another loud and violent fight

Lies and apologies all feel the same
Shattered hearts scatter the floor
   All red bloodshed,
    Another love dead

Monster

You are not a monster,
Just an unhealed soul
Searching for peace behind
The drama

You may have shattered hearts
On this journey,
But you don't deserve
To die lonely

You are worthy
Of healing,
Feed your heart
Some grace

Instead of pushing them away
Gently ask for space

Breathless

Holding my lungs

As I catch wind

On this wild journey

I want to feel

breathless while alive

Emotional Maturity

When you're mad
My first instinct
Is to adorn your weary heart
But I understand
it's best to give you space
To collect the words
You need to say
Instead of lashing out
In the heat of the moment
It's a blessing to share my life
With someone
Who's emotionally mature
Egos don't fuel
The fire to be right
We never curse or fight
We give each other space and time,
Then I hold you in my arms
As we talk it out

To The Heart I Broke II
(Before Closure)

I didn't know how
to kill softly
I was still a novice
At breaking hearts
So, I left without a word

I thought fading away
Was the easy way out;
I was a coward for dousing fuel
On the fire of doubt

Afraid to look into your eyes
and tell you why
We weren't working out

There was no way to tell you
I found someone else
Without making you
Think you weren't enough

A Day in 2037

Tomorrow's been canceled
Flashes cross the t.v. screen

A new plague
Swept the streets clean

Everyone sits at home,
To count the hours

Will it be a flood?
Will it be meteor showers?

We all knew this
Day would come
But why so soon

To spoil our summer,
Like hot milk,
Nothing blooms in June

The sun will go 'round
 For a final farewell

Hope there's heaven on the horizon
This planet has gone to hell

Nostalgia, Ultra II

Everything is so fleeting,
 I cling to every good feeling,
Like desperate fingertips
Slipping on the edge of a cliff

I don't want to let go,
the unknown is torture
Nostalgia is my drug of choice
I get high off reminiscing
refusing to sleep,
Don't wanna get trapped
In a dream

I'm aging too quickly; it seems
The world spins too fast
Under my feet

No control over time
Each moment, so fleeting
I try to capture all I can
Before the moment becomes distant

In the end, I'm left reminiscing

Tea

I won't sugarcoat my truth
To spare the bitter taste
It will leave in your mouth
If you're allergic to honesty
I'm not your cup of tea

Define: Toxic

The word *toxic* gets thrown around
Like old shoes, Worn down to the soles
Do people even know
what *toxic* means anymore?

No one is an angel
We've all caused damage
One way or another

Through the trials and errors of life
Many mistakes will be made
But redemption is a road paved
For those who are willing to change

(that's not toxic,
It's being human)

A toxic person
Is fully aware of
The error in their ways
But continues to cause
The destruction along the way

A toxic person creates an endless cycle
of chaos inflicted on its victims

A healing person tries to right their wrongs
To prevent themselves from becoming
A repeat offender

(***Be mindful of whom you call toxic***)

Be mindful of whom you call toxic. Sometimes, unhealed people do damage when they love because they have yet to learn how to be gentle with themselves. Maybe, the hurt they caused wasn't intentional; maybe it was a result of being emotionally immature.

I Ain't Mad at Cha

You did what was best for you
I'm happy about the change
You've grown so much.

Once close friends, now estranged
Feels so strange
Not having you here,
Your visions became the perfect picture
I just didn't fit the frame

Even though I miss you, I understand
You had to grow into ya own
There's no one to blame

Time has a way of
Changing the way we see things

(As Pac once said)

And I can't even trip,
I'm just laughin' at cha
You tryin' hard to maintain
But go ahead,
I ain't mad at 'cha

The Prayer III

Before you rest tonight, pray to those who hurt you. Pray they heal before breaking another soul. Pray they see with clear eyes when reflecting on their shady ways. See, it takes a great deal of strength to pray for the person who snapped your trust in half, but forgiveness is the key to healing. When you pray for them, you also protect the ones they encounter. ***Praying for them will send good karma back to you.***

When the time comes, forgive them for the emotional
bruises they caused, but don't allow them to rewrite history
When they claim your version of the story is wrong.

Emotional Bruises

The emotional bruises from my childhood are faint but still show in a different light, which means I've grown so much over time, but I still have plenty of healing to do.

<u>The Curse of Caring</u>

I wish I possessed
The ability to not
Give a fuck,
But I care too much

These emotions
Are easily affected
By the dark pollution
Surrounding me

I am not ashamed
Of this big heart
I feel deeply,
Even when the waters
Are shallow

But I do deserve a break
From caring too much

<u>The Decline</u>

My hands quiver
Like they're nude
Amid a brutal snow

And sleep becomes the enemy
When my nightmares call

I'm aware
my depression is near
Maybe a block away

I try to find a space
To feel safe,
But paranoia is 'round
The corner

Suppress my angst with a smile
While screaming inside

The slippery slope of
My mental health declining
Like a bad credit card

It's hard,
But when I need help
I don't hesitate to talk to
Someone I love

That's how I cope,
 I refuse to answer
When depression calls

Pretty Little Fears

I don't want to live
An empty life.
The pressure of success haunts me

Failure is the ghost
that lives inside my head

Sleeping next to
the shadows of tomorrow
I feel more alone than before
It entered my bed

When I waste time
Chasing behind the dreams
That taunt me, so daunting

To celebrate life
feels like a chore
Taking my sanity to the dumpster
Mopping my self-worth
Til my reflection shows on the floor

With all the strength I can muster
This self-inflicted punishment
How much can my heart endure
Before it cracks

Atychiphobia

Your fear of failure
Has handcuffed you
From trying at all
Imprisoned by excuses
You refuse to leave
Even when given the key

Then you cry to God
Questioning why
Life is so hard
When it's really your fault

Your blessings will not arrive
If you're too weak to push
Those fears to the side

<u>Young Abusive Love</u>

She was slender
With an ill temper
Quick to pop off
When I didn't
Fulfill her demands
My face--well acquainted
With her backhands

She'd play Ne-Yo's
When You're Mad
Like it was the soundtrack
To her madness

She loved me in a crazy way

We'd argue about her bad habits
Screw like rabbits
As she played Ne-Yo's
Make it work
Through the stereo
'Til her mom came home from work

She loved to play those damn songs
To say sorry for being wrong

She only struck me
Because she knew
I would turn the other cheek,
A one-sided boxing match
When I retreated in defeat

Chess Games

Manipulation was like a chess game to you
  Sneaking and cheating were the knights
  You played to blindside me
  Punching and fucking were the rooks
  You took to get ahead
  And I was the pawn
  Along with the other lovers
  On the board,

 Your lies were queen,
  The strongest piece
  You used to take all you could from me
  You knew how to foreshadow moves,
  Your trauma reigned king
   When you needed to siphon sympathy
   From me

Checkmate,
  You exclaimed before
  It was too late,
  With no moves to counter
  I was left empty
  And you had zero remorse
  After leaving my heart
  In pieces like a chessboard

<u>She Was a Virgo</u>

I was your first love
A truth you can't wash away
Like a wine stain
Forever embedded into
The fabric of your brain
  You will never forget me

Despite kissing your scars
To show how beautiful you are

I was the one left broken
To you forever was a moment
You left me with my heart frozen

When you said you loved me
Fear struck your heart,
Like lightening and life flashed
Before your brown eyes

You said I wasn't worth
Your time, you left without a goodbye

I gifted you
A special part of me
Just to watch you
Give it to someone else

No matter what,
You'll remember me
As the one
Who showed you how to love

There is no excuse for abuse
Don't fixate on
Protecting the person
Who is causing harm to you

(Some people can only see the brokenness within themselves)

They project emotional storms hoping you'll drown in the flood of misguided hurt. They see your path to healing as a threat when you liberate yourself from the same generational trauma they've been imprisoned by for so long. You're seen as the black sheep for seeking clarity; they call you every bad word under the sun, trying to burn every inch of love in what you call home. The truth is, they treat you like an outcast because they're empty inside. It's not your fault; you seek spiritual wholeness while they remain in the dark.

Sad Family Reunion

Depression is a ghost
That haunts your heart
When grief spreads
Wild like fire

It becomes more dangerous
When the mind festers
With unsettling thoughts

Sometimes it's patient
Because it strikes fast
Like a quick jab
When no one is looking

Unlike its cousin--- misery
Depression does its best work
On those who sit with it alone

Depression doesn't
haunt homes
Filled with love

<u>Scene: Action</u>

When you flipped the script on me,
And became victim to your own madness.
Using my empathy as a tool
To fix something beyond repair

For a while
  I thought leaving
     Would be a sign of weakness
How silly of me,
     to believe
Pain was a test of love

The Prayer IV

Dear Heavenly,

Please build me a warm home when I feel alone in this cold world. Give this place crystal windows so I can stare into heaven's soul when the sun glows. Build walls made of stone to keep the demons away. Fill this place with mindful and open people; make it a safe space with no judgments. Bless me with the sanctuary my heart yearns for.

Amen

Pinky Promise: If You Plan to Stay in My Life

Just know my heart
has been so spent
I can't afford
another disappointment,

(*So please,*
Be committed to your word
Be loyal to my trust
Vow that you will never deceive me)

If I put my trust in you
Can I rely on you
To keep it real with me
Even when it hurts?
Or should I prepare
For the worst?

Can I rely on you
To uplift my spirit
The weight of doubt
Holds me down?

If you plan to stay,
Promise you won't be quick to bail
When days get turbulent,
Life isn't always a smooth sail

I've entrusted my heart
With too many slippery hands
Can I trust you
to not break me again?

A Reminder:

Never toss salt on the sweet expression of affection. If the sight of a healthy love triggers a negative emotion, remain silent or walk away. Bitterness is an unsavory flavor. Your heartache doesn't give you the right to spoil anyone's bliss.

An hour without you,
Feels like a day without sun

Strings

Put my love in your arms
Use me like a guitar
Play me however you want
As long as
Your touch grazes the strings
Of my heart I don't mind,
Another you won't be easy to find

The Condition

You've been conditioned to believe
love is sacrificing parts of yourself
to make the relationship work

You think it's a constant tug and pull
 between egos and agendas, a never-ending battle
to see who gets the most by giving less.

You believe without hardships
 love is a farce, so you mock any notion;
that love can be soothing.

You have stopped believing in a healthy love
after so many turbulent heartbreaks;
every time you see any display
 of two people living in bliss,
 your first reaction is to call it a fairy tale.

You think throwing salt on
other people's sweet joy
because you're hurting inside.
A healthy love might be a fairy tale,
but fairy tales often come true.

Drenched

The clouds of grief

never cease to rain,

you just get used to

feeling drenched

Camera Roll

Random archives of your
Beautiful smile
Collecting dust
In my iCloud

Photo albums of you & me,
I'm reluctant to let go

As much as the pain aches
I yearn for the memory to stay

Pics of our first date, vacations,
silly selfies, and soaking in the sun,
Why would I want that to fade?

Gentle Reminders of a happier time
Before we drifted apart

Five thousand pictures of you,
Live on my camera roll,
Letting them stay
Is easier than clearing my phone

If Your Heart Could Talk, It Would Say:

Slow down. You're stressing me out. I deserve some rest after all the stress you're putting me through. You love hard, but you break easily, be more careful of who you spend energy on; I'm tired of being left broken and poor. I know you fear being alone, but desperation becomes depletion when you constantly reveal yourself to people who are not meant for you.

Loneliness becomes bliss the moment you fall in love with yourself. Discover who you are through solitude. The love you deserve will come after you resolve the conflicts--- tearing us apart.

Christian Mingle

Christians told me queerness
Is the opposite of God's light

An abomination of righteousness
And heaven's gates will never open
For God's bastard children

As I grew older
confusion blurred
The conflict of morality
What's right?
What's wrong?

What I did know,
I was never bullied by
A gay kid for being 'too weird.'
"Too soft', 'too goofy.'
Nor did they ever spread lies
On my name, like butter

No queer person,
made me feel like an outcast
I was never exiled by gay friends
For being myself,

As a straight kid,
I was betrayed by my own kind
For being an atypical black boy
I didn't fit in a box

As Christians told me to stay
Away from '*the gays*'

All I could do is wonder
How am I supposed to hate
The people who never hurt me?

Lust 4 Life

My addictions are healthier
than years before.
I no longer indulge
in self-destructive habits.

These days I enjoy writing on rainy days,
walks through the park,
 feeding wildlife,
people who fill my lungs with laughter,
mini road trips,
old-school music that's new to me,
good literature,
 and connections that inspire me.

My lust for life keeps me alive.

The Bull

Time is an impatient taurus

That waits for no one,

Take this day by the horns,

And brace yourself for a wild ride

Bask in the thrill of youth

Never fade into the age of worry

When the bull rushes at you

Don't fret; this moment is yours to take

The Angler

When casting your trauma
Into the ocean of my emotions
You knew how to use my empathy
As bait to reel me back in

You've mastered the art
Of using your pain
To gain this game
In your possession
To use me until you were ready
To toss me into the water again

But I was the fool,
For getting caught on your hook
After realizing the truth;
I'd rather drown alone
than to share air with you

People with the biggest hearts often find themselves learning their lessons the hard way for three reasons

1) We are more prone to give too many chances despite being exposed to who a person truly is. As a result, we suffer self-inflicted emotional abuse by setting out hearts up for disappointment.

2) We see someone's potential as a prize, so we wait for them to change to reap the reward. But, deep down, we know they'll never provide the love we deserve.

3) We treat our loyalty like a commodity when bargaining for reciprocity because we think we can build a future with people who live in the past.

(If you plan to stay in my life)

Be gentle with me,
Be patient too
There's a spot in my heart
That will forever remain soft for you

When you feel emotionally overwhelmed, be self-aware enough to know when to step away.

Resist the urge to use your tongue as a sword to puncture a hole into the person you love. Sometimes apologies won't patch the wounds inflicted by sharp words. Before saying something you will regret, ask for space, then talk it out when your emotions aren't so raw.

Treason

You are who you are

A kind soul with a giving heart

Too often,

You commit yourself

To leeches who drain

The life out of you

When the damage is done,

They slither to the next,

Leaving you alone,

to lift the weight of blame

Off your chest

 It's not your fault

Your only crime

Was keeping them around

for too long

Stop beating yourself up

Over their treason of trust

You must believe

You are not wrong

For being the kind soul

You are

On the other side of self-consciousness is pure bliss.
Once you stop worrying about what others think, happiness
will arise like a sunrise every time the mirror sees your
smile.

"After being starved for so long
You crave a love that fills
Your soul with trust and affection."

A Message to Your Situationship

Don't starve me of love
While feeding me empty lies
Do you really want to be mine,
Or am I wasting my time?

I know the truth isn't an entrée
On the menu
Just a sad date for two
In this venue

Your words are empty calories
They taste sweet but rot the teeth
When believed

So before I get full off you
Tell me the truth
Do you want me,
the way I want you?

I don't give full-time love
to part-time partners

Distant Lover

Raindrops knocking
On my window
As a reminder
That it's time
To start a new
I awake from the heartache
Of you not being here with me
While it's still dry
On your side of town
You sleep blissfully
As I reminisce
The last time you kissed me
You remain draped
In warm sheets
Dreaming of London
Dreaming of France
I wish I could meet you there
But I'm too far away
Just like when
you were next to me

Guilty Pleasure

We're not good for each other
But at night we're good to each other

Confusing lust with trust
 Emotions all mixed up
but we keep them bottled in
To protect whatever this thing is

    This affair we share
    Is a time bomb
    rapidly ticking
    Til it implodes

We know, but the future doesn't matter
when present pleasure
gives us a high no drug can replace

Wasting time feels good in the moment
Til one of us leaves the other
With their heart broken

Know when it's time to walk away

it's best to leave whole

than to break into pieces

while fighting to stay

High School Dreams

I dream of being back in high school
Far too often for my liking

I'm either
rushing through empty hallways,
Repeating senior year
despite earning straight A's,
On the football team
Being the star athlete I never was,
talking to the girl
I was too shy to speak to,
Sleeping in class,
Starting food fights

Those empty corridors haunt me,
Tainted by the bell's scornful tone
Urging me to hurry,
Because I don't have much time

Sometimes,
I'm the anxiety-stricken teen,
Trying to fit in
Other times, I'm my present self,
Just as lost as I was then

I keep dreaming of the four years,
I wish to forget,

The curse of an over-thinker…
over-dreamer

When I sleep,
my thoughts make
no damn sense
…but maybe there is a lesson to be learned

What void needs to be filled,
So these high school dreams can disappear?

You're Falling in Love Again

It feels like diving into the ocean
After forgetting how to swim

You take a leap of faith
Hoping their warm embrace
Will save you from drowning

Your last one was the opposite
Of a lifeguard, they forced you
To hold your breath
Under the deep cold water
they threw you in
They're the reason why
You're reluctant to trust again

But there is something about this new one
You're willing to give them a chance
Because their presence feels safe

They freeze the anxiety
bubbling in your stomach
making it easier to float
in love again
it feels so peaceful
when you swim in it

Maybe…hopefully..
this one is the one

Fear(Less)

You're not here to make everyone comfortable. You don't exist to please the world. Be loud. Be revolutionary. Be real. Be transparent. Be daring. You don't need to be the most liked. You just need to love yourself fearlessly.

Power of Doubt II

I wish I could see myself
Through your eyes
To understand how could
You love someone so damaged
And still handle with care

I'm beautifully broken
Like a rose after the storm

You are my sun
You see how wide I bloom
When I receive light
From you

Black Clouds

The next time those eyes rain
I hope you realize
Storms don't break you,
They give you the strength to grow
Dark clouds often pour
When they're needed most

Love Can Be

Silly convos
 through the bathroom door
   Binge-watching early '2000
    Tv shows

The 'What if we never met' game
  Goofy pet names,
    Snoring with no shame

Love can be
so wonderfully mundane

 Eating cookies past midnight
   Then promise to hit the gym
    To ease the guilt,
      But we both know it's a lie

     Pretending to be two
      actors on stage,
       Melodramatic plays we display
        To pass the day

Love can be so wonderfully mundane

 Stories of our childhood,
    Checking to see if the other is good
Even when six feet away
     Wasting an hour pondering
      Lunch and dinner for the day

  As thrilling and wild love can be
It's also wonderfully mundane.

Immature Love

The constant bickering over issues, with no effort to resolve them. Creating distance, being dismissive, only a knife can cut the tension when there's a lot of talk, but no one is listening.

Lying becomes a love language to ease the anger. You see a stranger when you stare into their eyes. You beg for candor, but they hide behind a disguise.

Losing sight of what you're fighting for, blinded by past happiness, trying to hold onto what you don't have anymore.

***Immature love is a like planting
 seeds in a wasteland,***
you can keep watering, but nothing will grow there
Understand, if they refuse to change,
Why are you so committed to staying with them?

<u>Dope</u>

It's so easy to fall into the trap of immature love,
 It's a new drug for empaths and healers.

We see immature love as a project or challenge,
 Hoping our influence can shape them into a higher form.

As lovers, we should help our partners grow,
But not at the expense of our sanity.

An immature love will drive you mad
when you try hard to teach them how to love you

It's up to you to decide if staying around is worth it.

The Prayer I

Dear heavenly.

Allow me to find solace amid the silence of darkness.
Protect my soul as I embrace this test of faith; I vow not to
break when life doesn't go my way. I'm aware this road to
self-discovery is a never-ending journey. Allow my
intuition to be a guide when my heart feels lost. I will find
my way, no matter the cost.

Amen

Pisces Heart

It's hard to disguise how I feel
My body speaks a language so clear
When my tongue refuses to move,
People can still read me.
Even when I move in silence,
my energy is loud

When I was younger,
I would tone myself down
to adapt to people around me

Now it's something
I'm proud of
There's no shame
in being emotionally transparent.

The Olympics

Trauma isn't a contest. There are no trophies for unfortunate events; to tell someone you've been through worse than them when they express their sorrow is a true display of dark character. Be mindful; we all conceal grief to mask yesterday's blemishes. Before trying to make trauma an Olympic sport, remember, like you, they carry pain too; some are better at being numb to it.

R.I.P

You're still alive but dead to me,
I tried to keep you close,
but you became a ghost
R.I.P to what we used be
You won't haunt me,
I'm at peace with your absence
I lost you and found balance
So don't come back,
stay missing like a picture
on the back of a milk carton
I won't go searching,
Or cry over your departure
Because the worst
thing you could've done
Was let me find out
How much better off
I am without ya'

Illusions

You're no longer easily manipulated
And this rubs them the wrong way. They view your growth
as a threat because the mind games they played to trick you
are too foreseeable to work now. ***Your eyes are too wise to
be fooled by the same illusions***. Not having control over
you makes them feel powerless, so they rush to change the
public narrative about you to swing the pendulum. Don't let
that knock you off your balance. You're in control; the
power belongs to you.

Losing You (oh)

I'm not bitter over losing you,
life became sweet the moment you left.

If you expect me to chase you,
 I apologize for the disappointment.

I refuse to waste energy
Running after someone
Who's committed to pushing me away

Your heart is a home
Stop letting them
Treat your love like
A revolving door

Affirm:

I am fluent in my love language,
I speak from my mind, body, and soul
Anyone who lacks the empathy
to understand my love,
will not be granted access
to my time

. When they push you away, don't beg them to stay
Fighting to be loved is the biggest waste
Of time, effort, and emotional space.

Sting

No matter how often my heart felt the sting of disappointment, I never spoke a love language that wasn't mine to keep someone around. My love language was foreign to some, while others lacked the comprehension to understand. I remained true to form because I knew someday my love would be the most beautiful language to the one made especially for me.

Common Sense

I desire to be seen,
Will the world open
Their eyes to me?

I yearn to be heard
I dread my voice
being silenced

I want to be felt,
I fear becoming
Comfortably numb

My heart wants to be
Be appreciated
My soul wants to be restored
With a life of substance

Righteous Love

You glow different when
You find a righteous love,

Be sure to stay true
To the souls who spark your light
And stay away from the spirits
That makes you feel dim.

Seed of Hope

Plant your last seed of hope
into the desolate soil,
Where dreams have been forgotten
How to bloom on this side of June,
Breathe air where life has no chance
Douse water onto land too dry to cry
One seed is all you need
To turn this wasteland into a home
You have the gift
Of growing gardens out of graves

Tough Love

I don't want tough love, struggle love, or dreadful love.
This soul is too pure for draining love, suffocating love,
listless- apathetic love.

My heart deserves to be fed transformational love. Tender
love. Generous love. When I gaze into your eyes, I need to
see transparent love. Liberating love, revitalizing love.

Please lead with empathy or leave me be.

Baby Steps

Healing requires patience
because it's not a sprint to the finish line.
It requires ten thousand baby steps
to meet your destination.
It's an ultimate test of faith.
Trust the process
and believe every step is worth taking

You are worth every second of effort
Every minute of affection, every hour of truth, and every
day of life.

The Game

Depression thrives when given the space to spread like cancer in your mind. Sometimes isolating yourself from the world is more dangerous than you think. When you feel empty---depression will use you as a canvas to paint its dark hues on. To sit alone with your sadness is playing right into depression's game.

No Desire

I have no desire to be in the presence of watered-down connections, dry conversations, and unseasoned minds. I've outgrown everything that doesn't enrich my soul. If the energy isn't pure, I can't be around it. If the love isn't revolutionary, keep it away from me.

Deep Pondering

And I would like to think
If you had the chance
To rewind time and come back
As the person who made me smile,
You'd do it within a breath of time

And if you had the chance
To erase the pain
To rewrite our final chapter
You'd hit backspace
Until the page turns blank

If life granted mulligans
I'd like to think you'd do the right thing

Because I still believe
In the tenderness-- you tried to hide,
I know there's still some compassion
Left inside

But since there's no going back,
Don't ache with regrets
You dealt the cards,
Now live with your hand

It took time to realize
I don't need you
to make amends or closure,
I'm strong enough
to heal on my own

Casting Call

I can sense phoniness from beyond a mile.
I know a bad actor when I see one.

My intuition is great
at weeding out the wicked souls
who've auditioned for roles in my life.

I'm protective of my space,
I can't share this stage with everyone.

When I find someone real,
I treasure the connection so deeply,
They become a star in my life

<u>ILY</u>

When I say, "I love you."
It's a testament
to my devotion to you

When I say, "I love you."
It's an agreement written
In the stars, so when
you gaze at the moon,
There will always be scriptures
For you

I say, "I love you."
As prayer to the angels
To keep you safe

I say, "love you."
To reassure,
You'll never consume another
Watered down love
My heart is pure

Tame

Tame your ego
before it gets too wild
You don't want to lose
the person you love
Over your foolish pride

Flume

Flow gently through my heart
Like water in a flume
Shine on my ripples
Like a river's moon
See the beauty
in my flaws too

I'm not broken,
Just an ocean
Of many moods

My temple is water
Dive into me
So I can replenish you

Vintage

I hope 40 years from
Now we're still
in our living room
With general hospital
And lifetime films
Over hot tea,
Enjoying each other's company
The way we should be

Perspective Pt I

"Where do you see yourself in 5 years?"

When asked 6 years ago
Alive was my response

The least I could've hoped for
beyond my depression
With no direction
I dwelled in a comfort zone
Submitting to my fear
of felling lost-alone

Lethargic every morning,
I had very little to look forward to
If staying alive was a win,
I was fine in the meantime

When depression found its way
Inside it controlled my life
I lost energy in my social battery
Sobriety became the enemy
I couldn't sleep.
I woke up dead… slugabed

Depression kills work ethic
I lacked motivation
I was content with staying *alive*

I wasn't sure if my life
Would still have light
In five years

<u>Perspective II</u>

"Where do you see yourself in five years?"
When people ask this today
I say, "alive."

Because when I open my eyes
I see a beautiful life
I don't want to miss a thing

Through the murky darkness
Of a healing journey,
I survived to see the light

From the flames
That tried to burn me
I discovered warmth
Amid the fire

In five years
I hope to be alive
I worked too hard
To die now

The fruits of my labor
Would rot too soon if I fade away
I deserve to enjoy the sweet life
After all the sour days
I've been through

Foolish Hope

You're tired of disappointment and confusion. Truth has become an illusion; you don't even know what's real anymore. When promises fly from their loose lips you know they won't land where loyalty lives. Yet, despite all the heartache you stay. Foolish hope leads you to believe they will change. How could you see a happy future with the person giving you hell today?

Relax Time

She's the destination,
A never-ending vacation
For this tired heart of mine
I worked overtime to earn
a love like this

Radical Love

The feeling
of emptiness disappeared
You filled my heart
With trust, clarity, and serenity

A once blurry life
became crystal clear
From the start
I stopped being my own enemy

Your infectious energy
Altered my being for the better
Your love is radical

They left you thinking they would find something better.
So don't be weak by taking them back when they try to
correct their mistake of pushing you away

Self-Preservation

Before I allow your ugly vibes to penetrate my peace of
mind, I will revoke your access to me. Blocking you will
bring me more peace than going back and forth with you.
Call me sensitive. You can even pat yourself on the back.
Either way, I'll be happier knowing I won't have to interact
with you again.

The Mortician

There are versions of me
Who won't see the light of day again
But I have yet to bury them away

I dress them up neatly
And gaze with a smile
as they receive the rest
They longed for

I inject the embalm
To keep them fresh
Open casket memories
flaws glow in all glory

No shame in their story
I'm in no rush to let them go

How could I host a funeral
For someone who still
Lives within me?

Afterglow

Like a sunset beyond snowfall
You give warmth,
When it's cold…
O how I revel
In your afterglow

I would never push you away
Nor would I ever let you go

People like you,
Are not easy to come by
I've never met anyone
Like you before
You are the most
beautiful soul I know

Afterglow II

She stands up
for the people
She loves
That's the way
her heart is set up

She believes
in her dreams
Despite the odds
 Her mind doesn't
Know the definition
Of giving up

There's no wonder
Why she attracts
Broken souls
They just want the chance
To bask in her afterglow

The Prayer V

Please restore my cup with calmness when anxiety disturbs my heart. Fortify my mind with the peace it desires. I'm ravenous for compassion; please fill my plate with the food for thought my soul needs; self-loathing is one unhealthy diet. I'm exhausted --- I'm ready to appreciate myself again.

Amen.

The Outlook

When your outlook on love is tainted, you begin to believe
a transformational love is unrealistic. After so much
heartache, love became synonymous with war, so pain feels
easier than peace. Instead of crowding your heart with
negativity, give yourself the space to heal from the trauma
of heartbreak. In due time, your perspective will shift, and
you'll realize a transformative love isn't impossible to find.
It starts with your mind; true love will discover you once
you believe in happiness.

Highway Crazy

You drive yourself crazy over someone who treats you like a pitstop when you are the destination. The more you show up, the less they appreciate you. You think those acts of kindness will be the key to their heart, but they see you as a pretty floormat to rest their feet on. The sad life of pleasing someone who takes you for granted will lead to wasted mileage on your heart. Don't let them wear out your tread, love yourself enough to know when to drive away.

For the Love of Rainy Days

What do you feel
At the sight of rain
Tranquility or pain?

Does your heart rumble
Like thunder when
The clouds inside you break
As your soul shakes?

When it rains
Where do you look,
Do you snuggle with a good book?

Two kinds of people
walk this earth,
the ones who find peace
when it storms
and the ones
who let themselves
drown under the downpour

Rihanna Ft New Edition

I will be the umbrella
To protect you from harm
When life becomes a storm
I vow to never let you drown
 If you can trust me with your pain
Together you and I will stand the rain

I Have No Title for This Poem

There's a place in your heart
That will never completely heal

A broken space ---vacant
desperately waiting
To be filled

But what if you need a little
Darkness to live?

What if that pocket of emptiness,
Completes you?

It's a gentle reminder
Of when life mistreated you

Maybe this part of you
Isn't meant to mend
Sometimes pain
Enhances your intuition

<u>Wake Tf Up</u>

The best part was watching the smug
Slowly escape your face
When I proved you wrong

Sleeping on me
Is a foolish thing to do
When I tell you who I am
Believe me

Open Heart Surgery

They weren't taught how
 to be soft and open-hearted
They keep you on edge
With a false sense of honesty

Transparency is a suit
They were never tailor-made for,
'cause showing emotion doesn't fit
who they are

It's not your fault,
Every time you climb those walls
They stack higher
To keep you away

You try to show them what life
Would be like
If they open their eyes
But darkness is all they know

They weren't taught
how to be soft
You can't open a heart
that's committed to being closed off

Need a Fixin'

Maybe that's how they learned
How to love at home

They might be the manifestation
Of the love from their absent parent
Or the parent who was apathetic to the situation

Blaming yourself ends today
You can't fix a broken soul
That came from a broken home

The best you can do is show them
That they don't have to heal alone

Fake Jewels

She's not easily fooled
By pyrite promises
She won't settle for
a cubic zirconia love

Her heart is not up for sale,
A woman who knows her worth
Won't waste her precious time
On anyone who tries
To scam her

Love is my motivation, love is my dream, love is what I strive to achieve, love is everything, love is me

4 A.M. affirmation

Don't trade your self-worth
For attention,
Don't barter your boundaries
For 'quality' time
Don't settle for their lies
Because the truth may cost
Too much

Love is not a bargain

Late Night Feels

I deserve a peace of mind,
I'm tired of arguing
with my inner voices
every night

It's The Voices

There's a war inside my mind,
The fight between calm and rage

The voices,

I never know which to believe

One speaks in a gentle tone
Providing the affirmative love
My soul starved for
The other voice —ugly and unstable
It tells me I'm a loser,
I'm not able

To overcome the hurdles
Placed on my path

Many fleeting voices visit briefly,
To put in their two cents
I never listen to what they say,
Nor do I remember

Each voice vies for my attention,
But I have very little to spare,

It's hard to find some peace of mind
When the voices never stop fighting

No Freeloaders

If they're going to live
in your mind every night,
they better be paying rent
Freeloaders can't occupy space
when you're trying
to build a home to heal in.

Euphoria

What you gave wasn't love,
It was a drug,

A euphoric sensation
For a short term
With lasting side-effects
Once done,

You had me duped for so long
I believed I wouldn't stand strong
Without your substance

I saw what I was becoming
Loving you felt numbing
So I went cold turkey

I'm sober of you now,
There's no chance of a relapse

I'm too wise to go back
to the time
I was emotionally high
Off your deceitful eyes

<u>The Light Again</u>

Once upon a time,
my mind couldn't fathom
a life without you.

Broken daydreams
of the moments we once shared,
I wish you still cared

Losing pieces of me
the keep you around
was an unfair trade,
when you left
my heart needed to be saved

But as the bitter aftertaste of your
demise waned,
I slowly realized
how well I could thrive
without you holding me back

I appreciate you
for leaving with your dark clouds
so I can see the light again

Rerouting

There's so much bliss on the healing journey ahead; stop
returning to the life that broke you. You will never find the
joy you deserve if you keep taking detours to the past.
Leave it in the rearview; if it's behind you, it's not for you.

Synergy

Such a beautiful feeling,
Energies intertwined
A harmonic chemistry
We bring each other
To a climax with just a stare,
This synergy we share
Our love is everything

The Talking Stage

The feelings you share
Before the situation gets too serious,
The thought of them
makes your heart spin

When you wake up
and your first instinct
Is to send a good morning text
You're so eager to see their face
You imagine a place
Where you're next to them

Every passing thought
Is consumed by
Their smile when they look at you
Or that goofy laugh
When you tell a cheesy joke
Or the way they dance
When they hear a good song

The little things,
You're allured by
You fantasize about a life with them
And time seems to move in slow motion
Because you can't wait to
begin your forever with them

The talking stage
Feels euphoric to a hopeless romantic,
But so slow ya roll,
Don't go chasing waterfalls
When you still have many rivers to go

The thrill of new love can be so enticing, but don't let the excitement blind you. Don't rush into something you're not ready for because you hate sleeping alone.

Just Like Music

What would the world
Be without you?
Your soul
Your story
Your rhythm
Your glory

You created peace
Where sanity couldn't be found

Joy was discovered through you,
Smiles were inspired by your style
Hope was restored through the soil
Of broken dreams

Because of your melody
Life shines through you,
The grand muse

People like you are
Just like music
A soothing tune
For souls looking
For a home to be listened to

The Chillz

Chill bumps cover my skin
Covered by a thin
Layer of sweat
My heart attempts to escape
The confines of my chest
My knees lock
My throat dries too

These thoughts, these fears
Are latching on like parasites
Feasting on my sanity.

I feel drained
But will I succumb?
Giving up is the easy route
Anyone can quit
the brave move forward

Die Alone

I feared dying alone
Until I realized
Living alone is better
Than dying from a love
That'll destroy me

The Giving Tree

Deep like the roots
of a tree no one has
the power to knock
me down

I stand tall ten toes to
the ground

I know who I am
I won't be pushed around

Rock solid
I'm still reaching
My peak

I shed fear like old leaves
You can hear my heart
When I speak

Deep---they see the growth
From the roots of this tree

Soft but not easily broken
I am a giving tree
My branches thrive in heat

Standing Ovation

You love them on borrowed time. When the curtains close
you will be left on this stage alone. You put on a
performance and bow for a standing ovation that will never
come. The crowd left years ago. The two of you have
drifted apart, but you'd rather sleep with a broken heart by
keeping each other around.

When will you drop the act and let them go?

Long Afternoon the Honeymoon Phase

They don't hold your hand
The way they did
When you two first met,
A soft gesture has become
A distant touch

Sparks no longer fly,
Your lips feel like strangers
When they meet.

They stopped making coffee
In the morning,
You forget to say goodnight

The bed is split in two
Silence feels more honest
Than talking

Quality time is a chore
You make no effort for anymore

It's past the honeymoon phase
When butterflies cease
To rise and you stare at them
With stale eyes

The only thing keeping this bond
Painfully close is the common fear
Of dying alone

Story:Time

I dreamt of a poem last night
The finest write of my life

This poem was a strawberry ocean
And a field of clouds too

Music notes flew
Through the wind's melody
Like canaries

No longer handcuffed by the rules
Of reality, this poem gave
My mind freedom

When I rose from my slumber
I grabbed the notepad to recapture
The magic I dreamt of

Just like most things beautiful
The words were too elusive to obtain

Instead of chasing
the poem of my dreams
I let it be free

If it's meant to be written
The words will come back to me

Weed & Melatonin

The only time sleep
Meets me halfway
These days

Most nights hours pass by
In the dark
My mind --more wired
Than a time bomb

I ponder about nothing & everything
At the same time
My body tosses in bed
Like pizza dough

I think about my next write
My next meal
And my last day of middle school

A million little things
Keep me awake

Weed and melatonin
Are the friends
That help me drift away
When my brain
Refuses to rest

Valid: Affirmation

My feelings are valid
My thoughts are valid
My love is valid
My dreams are valid
My expression is valid

I will stop apologizing
for being my divine self

(Things to Say After a Breakup Part 1)

I will always want the best for you, despite you being the worst for me. It's not in my heart to make an enemy out of someone I once loved.

(Things to Say After a Breakup Part 2)

No number of apologies will mend this broken bridge between us, so my condolences to the lover I lost. I'm sorry for putting you through hell despite being the angel I needed. You saw a sanctuary in me; I turned out to be the gravesite where the older versions of you were laid to eternal rest. *In loving memory of you and me…. R.I.P to what we used to be,* carved on the headstone. I was dead wrong; you were owed this apology long ago better yet, I should not have hurt you at all. I know I should save my breath because you no longer care. The irony of most apologies—they often come too late.

'

(Questions a Therapist Would Ask)

What stopped you from exiting this life? Was it hope? Was
it fear? What stopped you from making the pain disappear?

Was it the thought of your mother's cries
At the sight of your demise?

What is keeping you alive?
Share it with the world,
Don't hide

Tell us about the time
you saved your own life

Your story could save someone
Who has suicide on their mind

Empty

Your funeral is inevitable,
The scariest thing
About life is not knowing when
So, make the most of each day
Take the time to explore who you are
When the time comes
you will leave this earth empty
Your soul will rise with joy
Knowing you made the most
Out of your precious life

Transitioning

You are transitioning into the life you deserve. Some people don't find your growth flattering; they are not proud of the person you're becoming. Instead, they see your progress as a threat and will act accordingly. Do yourself a favor and create distance between the life you want and the people holding you back.

New Life: Gratitude

When you finally reach your mountain peak never forget the people who kept you up when you didn't have the strength to keep climbing. Give praise to the ones who gave you taith when you considered giving up. Thank the individuals who gave you new life when you felt like dying. No one can make it alone, so be grateful for the people who help you along the way.

The Walk

At the end of the day
It's about what you feel
Not what they think

Always follow your heart,
Not the opinions of people
Who've never walked in your shoes

There's beauty in emotional fluidity. Knowing when to settle down and let go is a special gift in a world where people take pride in being cold, toxic, or emotionally dense. Part of loving yourself is possessing the awareness to control your emotions while giving them the space to be free.

Truce

There's no shame in calling a truce
On the war storming in your mind
Sometimes waving the white flag
Frees your heart from the burdens
Holding you back
So you can begin the life
You deserve

Every battle fought,
Will not be won,
But the scars you acquire
Are blessings in disguise

You are a purple-heart soldier
An army of one.
As much as you've fought
You still stand ten toes down

There is nothing weak about you,
You have nothing left to prove

If you need to let go to move on
Do what you must
So, you can begin
The healing process

New Salvation

There's going to be a day
When your eyes will have no rain
Your heart will no longer beat with pain
And when you reflect on yesterday
Your mind won't be met with shame

This beautiful day
could be tomorrow
Or years away,
Either way,
You gotta stay alive to savor
The day you've labored for.

Never give up on your fate.
So much work was put in
To reach this destination

Don't waste it by
Leaving it all behind;
Please be patient with yourself

Your salvation is not far away

Timing

Falling in love after so much heartache
Seems daunting. You've become closed off
to the idea of falling for a new stranger, now you're over-
protective with your heart, and that's okay. Don't let
anyone pressure you into putting yourself out there again.
It's your heart, and you get to heal in your own time.

Stop repeating the same patterns
Make smarter decisions with your heart
If you're tired of being disappointed
Be careful of who you give your love to.
Dating is a process,
Not a race

If Laughter Was a Place

Nothing healthy for you
Is open 24 hours a day

The streets begin to clear
By 10 P.M

Anyone out past 11 P.M
Only looking for
A bad time with good intentions
A place to dance and drink
their demons away,
A place to fool around

If laughter was a late-night diner
What would they serve
The drunken and run-down,

Maybe lemon peppermint tea,
Waffles and eggs
A lil something to ease
the stress of yesterday,
No more hangover pain

This little place,
Would be an escape
For the sad souls
To fill their old bones
With new hope

Bonus Poems

Dust II

I write because I don't know
If I am a good writer yet,

So, I keep writing,
With the belief some
Good will come of it

Self-doubt is an art-form
I've spent 10,000 hours perfecting
At least I'm good at that

I don't know what good is,
I'm not sure if I'll ever be enough

I put words together
Hoping they make sense
To the world

Blank documents turn into
Reflections of my mind

Years down the road
When I look back at all the work
I've done
Hopefully, I won't care
about being good,
I just want to be proud

Poets are Not Therapists, Nor Gods

I can't fix your life,
Nor do I have all the answers
I'm flattered you think
Of me as a man with sage advice
But honestly,
I'm as young and dumb
As you are

That's the beauty
Were all frequencies
Experiencing life in different phases

Personally, I'm not going
To tell you what to do,
I'm not a life coach or therapist
But with these words
I will spark the brain
To ask the questions
You've been hiding from
Your whole life
So you can unveil the answers
On your own

My job is to inspire
And challenge you
Even when it hurts

You may read poems like scriptures
But I promise no poet is a God

Poems are good for the soul
But don't devout your life
Like it's a religion

So please stop asking me
for relationship advice.

A Home for Lonely Souls

(You probably already know the answer)

If you need advice
on how to stay alive;
I urge you to call 9-8-8

Don't seek me
When you want to quit school or your job
(Ask your bank account)

Poetry is a gateway to healing,
but it's not an all-purpose tool for fixing,
When a good poem
Touches your heartstrings
Ask the questions your heart needs to hear
Then go seek the professional help you need

The Zoo

Behind my apartment building
Stands scraping trees
With ever-changing leaves
For each season,
A large ditch of wild emerald

Many species made
This place their home
A skunk and his son,
A family of groundhogs,
Chipmunks. Squirrels. Raccoons
Deer and foxes come to visit here and there
Turkey vultures
And a dozen other birds too…

The old man, Fills the bowls,
With food and water
And scatter sunflower seeds
over the grass for the birds

I often serve the groundhogs
Freshly cut fruit

When the sun isn't too cruel
I stand on my deck
And watch the animals
Fill their bellies,

Taking their turns,
No shoving or punching
Or bogarting food for themselves

They're all aware that
There's enough food
For all of them to eat

Why can't humans be the same way?

The Stray

The feral feline,
Who resembles Garfield
Wanders outside my
apartment building,

"He's a rolling stone,"
the old man says

 Garfield visits his kittens
And feasts off the food
given to them by the old man
Who cares for the litter
When he makes his rounds
I wonder where he settles
When he leaves

"He's been homeless for 8 years,
ya know,"
The old man shares.

A cat without a home
He's survived fire and ice
Hurricanes & Raccoon fights
I'm sure he's outlived nine lives

A strike of sonder,
Lit my eyes,
Once I realized
This cat has lived

One extraordinary life,

I wonder if he brags
About his adventures
To his kittens,

The way I'll share my story
With my children

Duck Feeding

A school of 'em
Quacking and waddling
They gawk with their beady eyes

I toss a handful of seeds
Into the air. And watch 'em
Feast, I throw more and more,

They surround me like
I'm their God,
They grow louder
I can't tell if they're
Angry or praising me

I throw the last batch and run away,
This time they're not plucking the ground
They're chasing me,
Barking like dogs,

I've been rushed by far worse,
This was light work,

I was able to elude them
once I crossed the field,

That made me smile,
I'll wear better shoes next time

Her Rapture

I fell in love with you on accident
Like a heavy accent
I could barely understand
Why were you put on
My axis now I'm spinning- smitten
Caught up in yo rapture
Like a pastor
You holla what my soul needs
After A life of sinning
I'm repeating,
Your type of love
Is the permission
To be forgiven huh

My life was a storm
You helped weather it
I didn't need saving
You helped better it
Like a feather,
You gently fell into my lap

There's no going back
to the lonely loathing soul
I used to be
When I dream
I see you and me

Final Note

When the eye in the sky
Rains upon you
Let downpour
Drench the pain away

The Water will replenish
The desolate space
Festering in your soul

I hope the words have helped you. I hope these words have shed light on the dark place inside you. With that said, the work doesn't stop here; if you or someone you love needs emotional support, seek professional help. Below is a list of resources you can use and refer to others,

Hotlines:
Suicide prevention hotline: 988
Addiction Abuse Hotline: 888-307-4010

Apps:

Better help (for professional 1-on-1 therapy)
Calm (for daily meditation)
Talkspace

Printed by Amazon Italia Logistica S.r.l.
Torrazza Piemonte (TO), Italy

51592979R00121